For Evelyn Rose and all her cousins... and for Phyllis Naidoo and Martha Mokgoko and Luli Callinicos,
grandmothers sowing seeds of change for South Africa's children – B.N.
To Lisa, Katlego and Bojanara in Cape Town; Jumbo in Durban; Mr Osburn,
staff and pupils of Greenside Primary School and Mrs Vanzeeburg, Mrs Peter, staff, pupils and parents
of Parkview Junior School in Johannesburg for their kind support;
to Evashini for her invaluable advice, and to Janetta, Judith and Yvonne at Frances Lincoln
for sharing my enthusiasm for South Africa – P.D.

S is for South Africa copyright © Frances Lincoln Limited 2010
Text copyright © Beverley Naidoo 2010
Photographs copyright © Prodeepta Das 2010
The Publishers wish to acknowledge Ifeoma Onyefulu as the originator of the series of which this book forms a part.
Ifeoma Onyefulu is the author and photographer of *A is for Africa*.

First published in Great Britain in 2010 and in the USA in 2011 by
Frances Lincoln Children's Books, 4 Torriano Mews,
Torriano Avenue, London NW5 2RZ
www.franceslincoln.com

The Publishers wish to thank the following for their assistance: Maren Bodenstein,
Jean Williams and Biblionef, South African Mobile Library Association, Robin Malan, Ncumisa Mayosi,
Greenside Primary School and Parkview Junior School in Johannesburg, Modikwa Primary School in Limpopo Province,
Rathfern Primary School, London, the Maharasingham family, Madeleine Lake, Maya Naidoo, Charlie and Lucy Hill.

A catalogue record for this book is available from the British Library.

ISBN 978-1-84780-018-3

Set in Vega Antikva

Printed in Shenzhen, Guangdong, China by C&C Offset Printing in March 2010

1 3 5 7 9 8 6 4 2

S is for South Africa

Beverley Naidoo
& Prodeepta Das

F

FRANCES LINCOLN
CHILDREN'S BOOKS

Author's note

The Republic of South Africa is a huge country at the southern end of Africa stretching from the Atlantic to the Indian Ocean. Travel across it and you'll be amazed at how the land changes from golden beaches to forests, deserts to grassland, valleys to mountains. You will find many different plants, birds, animals, people, languages, religions and kinds of music. We have three capital cities: Pretoria (our government headquarters), Cape Town (our Parliament) and Bloemfontein (our Supreme Court).

When I was a child, our beautiful land was made ugly by racism. Black, brown and white people were forced apart by apartheid (separateness) laws, and children of different colours weren't allowed to go to the same schools or live next to each other. Many brave people protested against this and went to jail. Many sang songs about the jailed black leader, Nelson Mandela. They cried tears of joy when he came out of prison. He became South Africa's first black president in a government elected by people of all colours in 1994.

It's not easy to change a country that has been so unequal and unfair, but our "rainbow nation" children are calling for change. Yebo! Yes, we can!

Beverley Naidoo

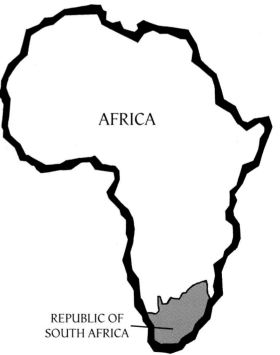

 is for Apartheid Museum
showing all the hate in our grandparents' past,
black and white forced apart.
But now, hand in hand, we invite you to our land
and declare, "Let's build a country for all of us to share."

Bb

is for Bunny Chow.
My tummy is rumbling.
I say to the lady,
"A quarter beans, please."
She cuts a quarter loaf of bread
and scoops out the middle.
Feeling brave, I add, "Extra hot!"
She spoons spicy bean curry
into the hole, while my tummy
murmurs, "Hurry! hurry!
Put that bread-lid back on top!"
Soon my fingers and mouth
will sink into my Bunny Chow.
If you could see me then, wow!

is for Cricket and crazy friends steaming in on sticky wickets,
striking a slog – a slash – a slice – skying the ball to a fielder.
Yoh, it's a donkey drop! A dolly! A duck! Bowled out, bad luck!
My friends dream of playing Test Match tours…
"Watch us! We're South Africa's future 'Proteas', for sure!"

is for Days on Durban beach, its sunny shores open to all.
Soccer is our passion and we love to kick a ball.
If we want to swim or surf, no need to fear the sharks –
there are underwater nets to keep us far apart.
Then, safely back on land... we'll carve fierce dragons in the sand!

E e

is for Every child
whose tummy is empty.
On icy nights
they make fires,
warm hands and toes,
whisper, *"Eish,* it's cold!"
huddle up like puppies,
sleep under a bridge,
dream of making music,
money for fancy haircuts
and tickets to take the train home.
In Soweto you see them painted
on this huge cooling tower –
no longer used for making power.
But in our cities and our towns
life is tough for real children living rough
whose only friends and family are each other.

is for Faces, ancestors from many places
with stories to share of one human race.
Let all our children be laughing and peaceful,
and understand the wisest saying of our rainbow nation:
"People are people through other people!"

Gg

is for Gold and eGoli – city of Jo'burg!
Your gold gleams like butter on a red plate.
But imagine... down in the dark,
deep underground,
feet pound to the sound of men
wrestling with rock
to dig out the gold that built a city –
and in villages far away
children wait for the day when fathers
come home safe from eGoli.

eGoli means "Place of Gold", the isiZulu name for Johannesburg

 is for Homes and Hoping for a future
where every child has shelter
with warmth in winter, water to wash
and somewhere safe to play.

is for Imbira,
my little piano.
My thumbs twing
and you sing!
Aiee, my little friend
from Zimbabwe!

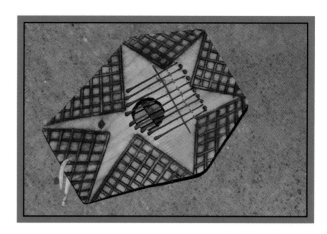

is for Jewellery.
Bright beads,
nimble fingers
and thread
are all I need
to make a bracelet
for you to wear.
Come and try it!
Come and buy it!

K k is for Kubu. Stop and stare. "Great fat hippo!" you jeer and peer.
See me slumbering, lazily lumbering, but beware!
Annoy me – dare me to run –
before you say "hippopotamus", you'll feel my fine teeth, eheh!
Now, that will be fun!

Kubu is the Setswana word for "hippopotamus"

 is for Library, lost in a story,
curled up on cushions in the corner.
"Once upon a time... Long, long ago... Yesterday..."
Sometimes, when we step inside,
we don't want to leave!

Mm

is for Madiba – Nelson Mandela!
Madiba, elder of your clan.
With friends, black and white,
sent to prison for life
you fought for everyone's right
to be equal and free.
After twenty-seven years
your jailers tired of war
and unlocked your prison door!
Madiba, our first President
elected democratically,
your words still ring urgently:
"Let's share our land in harmony."

 is for Ndebele house-painting,
taught by mother to daughter.
No rulers for straight lines needed here!
How skilfully hand and eye show land and sky
and secret signs unknown to passers-by.

is for Our dream.
We stitch the words
EDUCATION IS LIGHT.
Through work and play
we dream to unite.

is for Protea,
our famous flower
named after Proteus,
shape-shifting god of the sea.
Remember this, when you watch
our cricket team 'The Proteas'
live up to the fame of their name!

Qhina is the isiZulu word for "plait"

is for Qhina.
Plait my hair in a style
that turns heads
and makes me feel like a queen!
I'll sit here all day so you can work your wonders.

R r

is for Roadside seller.
See how patiently she sits
sorting her wares.
Green bananas today
and spinach leaves.
"Fresh, fresh!" she'll say,
without telling you
how far she has trekked
with her bags on her head –
setting out in the dark before dawn,
returning at night after sundown
to eager children who greet her:
"Mama, what did you bring from town?"

S is for South Africa where two oceans meet,
cold Atlantic from the west and warm Indian from the east.
Our country stretches wide over Africa's southern shores
from golden beach to misty mountain, desert sand to grassy plain
in a land of contrasts where we praise the sun – yet pray for rain!

is for Table Mountain
towering over Cape Town, city and bay.
When the South-Easter blows,
cotton-wool clouds billow and grow.
"See the giant's tablecloth!" people say.

is for uMama and our mothers who give us life.
Our grandmothers remind us how they marched for their rights,
how, in jail, they drowned the sound of keys jangling in the lock
with their singing, "When you strike a woman, you strike a rock!"

is for Voices. We raise them high.
"Lift the roof!" says our teacher,
"Let's reach for the sky!"
"Nkosi Sikelel' iAfrika," we sing,
"Lord Bless Africa," our national anthem.

is for Wildlife in the bush, where many species thrive.
Elephant, Buffalo, Leopard, Rhino and Lion are our Big Five.
We treasure nature's wonders, great and small, in game reserves –
for future generations they must be cared for and preserved.

is for isiXhosa. I speak it at home –
it's easy for me to click!
South African languages weave like a song:
isiZulu, isiXhosa, Afrikaans,
Sesotho sa Leboa, English, Setswana,
Sesotho, Xitsonga, siSwati, Tshivenda,
... and, don't forget isiNdebele!

is for Yebo! Yes! Yes!
We can feel it in our fingers.
You can see it in our eyes.
Yebo! Yebo! Yes, we can!

is for Zoo Lake in Jo'burg, our "Jozi".
We picnic in families, hang out with friends.
The ducks say hello – they are always so nosey!

It's sad to have to say goodbye,
but come back to South Africa's great open sky!
Go well! *Mooi loop! Hambani kahle!*

Mooi loop! and *Hambani kahle!* mean "Go well!" in Afrikaans and isiZulu